Come
Sit
Awhile

GESTALT PHENOMENOLOGY

SIERRA "THE MORNING STAR"

Integrity Publishing
39343 Harbor Hills Blvd Lady Lake,
FL 32159

www.integrity-publishing.com

CONTENTS

INTRODUCTION

My pen name is Sierra "The Morning Star". The morning star is in reference to my Maya/Aztec Astrological Venus Phase: Morning Star. A meaning of the term morning star is shining bright light.

A translation of Sierra is high jagged/saw tooth mountains. Mountains are high and therefore relational to other terms of height, i.e. celestial. The term celestial can also be associated with love and produce the term celestial love, and a translation of that term, highest love. To me the highest love is self-love or the very love of self. Self-love is not selfish love. It is a love that cares for oneself but not at the expense of other people.

To me the pen name Sierra "The Morning Star" means celestial bright shining light of love.

PROLOUGE

I began my spiritual quest earlier in life than most. My father and sister died untimely deaths six months apart when I was eleven years old. She was sixteen, five years older than me. She awoke sick on Saturday morning (March 27, 1965) with flu-like symptoms. My parents called the doctor and he said, "If she's not better Monday morning bring her into the office, in the meantime give her plenty of fluids and aspirin for her headache." She died at home in my father's arms on Monday morning (March 29, 1965). Her greatest concern before the ambulance arrived was to change her underwear. She didn't want to go to the hospital in the pair she was wearing. The autopsy revealed she died of a rare virus that eats the heart. They don't know where it comes from or how one gets it. It was the first recorded case in Washington County, Pennsylvania. My Mother and Father never forgave themselves. They felt there was something else they could've should've done. My father two years earlier had open heart surgery, a plastic aorta valve; he was just beginning to feel better when my sister died. He constantly questioned why her, why not him. Within the next six months my father's quilt and unacceptance of her death created so much stress on his brain he had a cerebral hemorrhage. He got a stiff neck and headache but didn't go to the hospital for days. He fell into a coma shortly after being admitted to the hospital and died on a Thursday morning, at the age of 42, in late September of 1965.

I was left with my mom, but really left alone. She was consumed with her grief and was incapable of helping me with mine. My father's family disappeared and most of my mom's. What once had been a home filled with laughter, family and friends became empty and silent.

My dad was a shift rolled steel worker at one of the steel mills near Pittsburg, PA. He had been my confidant. He taught me how to do everything. Swim, fish, camp, ice skate, sled ride, ride my bicycle, cut the grass, use a weed sickle, garden, cook, bake, pump out (in the spring); cement, paint, fill, run the filter, fix the filter, skim, check the ph balance and vacuum our in-ground swimming pool. He taught me how to fix the stockade fence and ensure the gate was locked each evening when I was done swimming. He taught me how to love other people, to be accepting, to be courageous, to be courteous, to believe in myself and to be self-sufficient. Little did I know it was because he wasn't going to be here with me. As a young child he allowed me to slide down the windshield on his car, to sit on his knee as he drove, he took 8mm movies of me every day before I went to kindergarten and made sure someone picked me up every day at lunch from school. He watched Tarzan with me every Saturday morning and Saturday Night at the Movies every Saturday night. On Sunday evenings, as I sat on his lap for many years, we would watch the Walt Disney show "The World is a Carousel of Color, Wonderful Wonderful Color". When I had the measles and couldn't see because they were in my eyes, he sat and explained to me what was happening on TV.

I never knew my sister as a person. I was the little sister and she was always trying to get away from me and pushing me out of her life. Such is the five-year age difference when siblings are young. She was very smart. I remember one evening watching her break pencils at the kitchen table. She was making a guillotine for her Marie Antoinette project; breaking the pencils in half and removing the lead for the razor blade to slide down. I also remember a project she did on Mary Queen of Scots. She had friends, but she didn't have the opportunity to go on a date. It was a tradition at her high school for the sophomores to serve at the Junior/Senior Prom every year, her sophomore year she was an Italian waitress. I remember her off the shoulder peasant shirt; she looked very beautiful in it. I remember it being very exciting for her.

My Mom taught me to work hard. Every weekend we did a different project; one Saturday we would take down all the curtains in the kitchen and dining room; wash them, hand towel dry them, then iron and hang them before dinner. The next Saturday all the kitchen and dining room chairs would be turned over, the legs, underneath the seat, and foot stands cleaned; another Saturday while we were washing clothes, I would help scrub the cellar floor and, hang clothes to dry; inside in the winter, and outside in the spring and summer. Another Saturday we would wash baseboards, the next the walls. Once I helped strip old wall paper off the walls, it was fun. First, we soaked the walls with hot vinegar water and peeled layer after layer of old wall paper: roses, ferns, multiple-colored flowers.

My Mom and I weren't very close emotionally. She was the one that scolded me. However, she always told everyone I was perfect, and she told them all the time. Here I was alone with my mother, someone I really didn't know very well, odd huh? We grew more distant emotionally as she struggled through each day with her own grief and emotional pain. She didn't know how to help me and she didn't know how to help herself. She had had my dad to see her through and now she was alone too. She was my mother and she loved me and I had a place to sleep and food to eat, I was physically safe…. but I was alone, my whole being ached and life was never the same again.

At the age of eleven I began to pursue the meaning of life. What are we here for? What is it all about? What are we supposed to do? Where does it all lead? And if death is the destination for us all what is the journey for? What could we all possibly be here for, loving, laughing, learning, living if the result was death? Was this some bizarre circumstance we all found ourselves? Was there really no purpose to it all? Does how we approach life matter if the result is death?

Many times, I was asked by others who were grieving, "When does the pain go away?" My answer was, "The pain goes away but it never stops hurting."

I do still grieve for them and I don't think that will ever go away, but I can say the physical pain has gone, it has stop hurting, but the essence remains. Perhaps it is a unique process for everyone.

My first experience with Psychics was at a Spiritualist Community near Daytona Beach, Florida in 1987/1988, age 35. At my first reading I was asked, "Do you want me to start with your present, past or future?" I said, "My past." I was going to use the information the reader gave me to verify the authenticity of the reading. And to my surprise I was astounded. The first words out of her mouth were, "I shudder to see the death that surrounds you." (my father and sister died six months apart March of 1965, then September of 1965, then one of my mother's twin brothers age 31 died in July of 1966 in a car accident on the way home from work). Then she said," Whose Pam", I said, "My sister, she's dead." The reader said, "She wants you to know you can do this yourself." The reader also told me I was an ancient soul. That we had all been here many, many times, but I had been here thousands upon thousands of times. This particular information was given to me two more times, at my first palm reading and then my first astrological chart I had created. In an astrological chart there is a certain symbol that appears when the soul being charted is one of the ancients. This is one piece of information I have yet to receive 100% clarity as to what exactly it means to be an ancient. Except that it may explain why I understand everything so very differently and why I experience life very differently in very different ways from everyone I meet.

So, I began my journey into the spiritual realms of information gathering. I saw several different readers from the spiritual community but one I met with many times throughout the next thirteen or fourteen years. I was having a reading done by another reader from the spiritual camp community. She said to me, "Your father and sister died untimely deaths," I said, "Yes", and explained to her what had happened. I added, "My father and I did everything together, I was my Daddy's little girl," and she replied, "But he's with her isn't he?" That knocked me off my feet so to speak. She said they had had many lives time's together as, brother and sister, father and child, mother and child, husband and wife etc. and that is why when she died, he died so soon afterward, it's their choice to always be together. Once I was over the initial shock, of receiving this information, I think perhaps this was when the pain started to go away.

One Saturday morning after my sister died, I thought I saw her in the bed next to me. I called to my father to come quickly but he kept delaying saying he would be there in a minute. When he finally came into the bedroom, he told me my sister had come to visit him. That she laid her hand on his chest to heal his heart. When he had his next checkup, his physical heart was completely healed. She had been there. She was still earth bound because she was waiting for him. Of course, at the time I was eleven and all this just frightened me!

What I knew at age 11 was there was more to being on this planet than most humans were aware of and were even interested in understanding. I knew deep within my being there was more and that something big was in the que, something that had never happened before a time in space that was a destiny for humanity and our planet, but I couldn't find evidence that anyone else felt this, anticipated it or was willing to acknowledge it. When most teenagers view themselves as immortal I was searching at great depths within and without for the answers to the meaning of existence. I was raised in the First Christian Church Disciples of Christ which taught me to live my Christian beliefs in my everyday life. My journey into metaphysics goes way beyond the teachings of the Christian religion I was raised in. To me one of the most important metaphysical concepts is eternal life means a real existence in another space. A space we cannot get to in our physical bodies but a very real place. A space where we learn, a space to prepare to return to earth to learn what cannot be learned without taking on a physical body.

In the early 90's I bought a house on Cocoa Beach. I would run on the beach in the evening after work and on the weekends. Sometimes I ran 42 miles a week but most weeks it was between 18 and 24. I was never sure if it was the ocean or the running that prompted my subconscious to open and journey forward or perhaps it was preordained. The visions began then and almost like an in- between. Somehow a vortex was created in my front living room window off the screened porch. At night tall spindly angels would enter as I fell asleep to begin the teachings of what I had forgotten and prepare me for what I was to learn.

Over the next several years I had many physical spiritual experiences. Once I was driving a government vehicle flying down Interstate 4 in the left lane (of course obeying the speed limit) on my way to Lakeland, Florida to perform a work function. I started to get this wonderful feeling in my chest that continued to expand. I was thinking, I'm so glad I ran last night I feel so wonderful! Then in the center of my chest there was this starburst feeling, I could see the starburst in my mind's eye or soul eyes and I could feel another being layered over me. It was as if my chest had opened up and my soul had expanded outward around me and was helping me hold on to the steering wheel. I was trying to process all this when I heard scrap, scrap, scrap. I realized it was the tire rim scrapping the road and that I must have a flat tire. I pulled over to the right lane and off on to the shoulder. When I got out of the car to look it was the front right tire and it had been completely blown off. The being that surrounded me was me, my divine self and the wonderful feeling in my chest divine love.

I continued my search for a group with the same metaphysical concepts I embodied. I bought books at the metaphysical book stores at the Spiritualist Camp I frequented and found a group on the internet. I read all the books that contained channeled information from a particular entity and attended a channeled seminar in Orlando, FL. This group had a website and on that website was referenced two other groups. I resonated in particular with one of those groups and began to attend seminars presented by that group. I had found the information I had been looking for, but what I didn't realize was it was the channeled information I resonated with not the humans, even though they considered themselves to be highly evolved spiritually. The information being channeled was the information I had been seeking. It was interesting for me from month to month to listen to the channels because the information being channeled was what I had experienced the previous month.

The poems in this book reflect metaphysical and personal insights of my journey and of my daughter and grandchildren. I hope you enjoy reading them as much as I have enjoyed creating them.

Gestalt Phenomenology is a problem-solving methodology for personal, business, organization or spiritual, issues/problems/opportunities for improvement or goal setting. It's based on the concept of the configurated whole, a Gestalt, and the interrelationships that exist in a configured whole and the effect those relationships have on each other in the problem-solving process.

GESTALT PHENOMENOLOGY

**"The Essence of the Experience as
It Relates to the Configured whole"**

INTRODUCTION TO
GESTALT PHENOMENOLOGY

Gestalt Phenomenology as an integrative and inter-relational problem-solving/information gathering methodology. It can be applied to many circumstances i.e. business/organizations/government, personal and spiritual challenges/issues/opportunities for improvement.

Gestalt is a German word that means a configured whole. At its' center or heart, is the essence of the experience, how the experience made you feel.

A configured whole is how somethings' parts are put together in a particular form or arrangement. The parts of a configured whole are interactive and inter-relate to/with each other. To understand the whole, you have to identify the parts.

Phenomenology is a descriptive or classificatory account of the phenomena of a given body of knowledge without any further attempt at explanation. From a business/organization/government standpoint the problem-solving/information gathering methodology can be used with integrated process-based management systems; on a personal level it can be used as a Life and Spiritual Coaching methodology i.e., as a guide through the grief process.

The methodology is:

1. Define the problem/situation/challenge/opportunity for improvement
2. Ask Why (as many times as you need to)
3. Create a time line of events
4. Identify mitigating circumstances
5. Collect information (data gathering)
6. Analyze the information
7. Develop an action plan - Execute the action plan
8. Identify lessons learned

GRIEF APPLICATION

Gestalt Phenomenology as an integrative and inter-relational problem-solving/information gathering methodology. It can be applied to many circumstances, including Spiritual Coaching/ Counseling.

How each of us works through grief is a unique personal/spiritual journey. There are many things that cause us as humans to grieve but they are all related to loss. The loss of a job, a friend, a divorce, betrayal, a loved one.

To me the most important thing to know about loss is that it is to be grieved. Loss is physically, emotionally, psychologically and spiritually painful. We are human and grieving is how we survive loss. If the loss is severe enough, we grieve the rest of our human life. This is not as tragic as it sounds for grief can be a motivator to accomplish things, we thought we were not capable of accomplishing or things we would never have thought to pursue. Grief can make us fearless! However, the pain of deep loss never goes away, it stops hurting eventually and is replaced with a kind of numbness where the pain existed. The numbness feels like an empty space in the center of your chest.

We have the choice to allow grief to destroy us or make us more curious, more motivated, more open to all that is available to us. To pursue paths of thought and experience we would otherwise of, been blind to, ignored or thought to be irrelevant.

Perhaps one of the first things we do when we experience loss is ask, why. Sometimes we know the answer but we still question, why. Did I do something wrong, say something wrong? Was I not good enough? We look for a way to blame our-self rather than accepting maybe, just maybe there were mitigating circumstances we were unaware of, or the other person was acting on their behalf and it had nothing to do with us. Never accept someone else's blame but always know you are accountable for your behavior and your actions and how you respond to some else's behavior/actions.

Did you lose your job, friend, spouse, were you betrayed? Did you lose your job, friend, spouse because of your behavior or someone else's behavior or mitigating circumstances you were unaware of? Take accountability for your behavior and acknowledge you are not responsible for someone else's behavior. I have found the old adage "when one door closes another one opens", to be true, but you have to be receptive to the idea that the new door that opens may be a door you never opened before, be ready for new opportunities and experiences, be ready to learn!

If it's important enough to you to explore further than asking why, you can create a timeline of events that lead to the loss; identify mitigating circumstances related to the loss; collect data regarding the loss; analyze the information; develop an action plan, so for your part it doesn't happen again (you don't repeat the same mistakes) and; identify the lessons learned from this loss.

Don't stay in the past! Move your-self forward with honesty and integrity! Learn to know yourself! Release the pain and move forward because the only way out is through!

In grieving for the loss of a loved one, most of the time the reason the loved one moved on to the other side of veil was because it was preordained before they were born. It was not to sadden or punish you. The loss of a loved one is very painful and difficult to accept. Honor the time you spent with them and celebrate remembering them.

The methodology can be followed and perhaps provide more information to you to guide you through your grief: create a timeline of events that lead, up to loss; identify mitigating circumstances related to the loss; collect data regarding the loss; analyze the information; develop an action plan to move forward with your life; and identify the lessons you learned from this loss.

Don't stay in the past! Move your-self forward with honesty and integrity! Learn to know yourself! Release the pain and move forward because the only way out is through! You have your life to live! Love and celebrate your life, even if at first you are only going through the motions!

Gestalt Phenomenology is the essence of the experience as it pertains to the configured whole and can be used as a Life Coaching/Spiritual Counseling Model to solve/resolve personal issues.

ORGANIZATION/
BUSINESS APPLICATION

A configured whole can refer to a Quality Management System, business system, such as ISO 9000 or AS9100 or, any business system or a government structure such as a Democracy.

A Quality Management System can provide a structure to use the integrative/inter-relational problem-solving/informational gathering methodology of Gestalt Phenomenology for business and technical issues. Government structure of the configured whole would be i.e. the Constitution and Bill of Rights of The United States of America, which in America are the laws that create the rule of law, social norms and values for the citizens in the US.

A configured whole can be a subset of a larger whole. Like a technical issue or a business or Government process or department. The whole can be the subset of a larger whole.

To resolve an issue/situation/event, the configured whole of the problem as it exists, must be examined for interrelated activities to determine why the situation/problem/issue/opportunity for improvement exists and how to solve it. All causes/links (supplier, inputs, process, outputs, customer) that contribute to the situation/issue/event must be identified and resolved so the root cause can be identified and corrected.

Define the Problem/Goal/Situation/Issue

Ask why, is this a problem; why do I want this goal; why did this situation develop occur; why is this an issue?

List the following:

1. Define the problem/situation/challenge/opportunity for improvement
2. Ask Why (as many times as you need to)
3. Create a time line of events
4. Identify mitigating circumstances
5. Collect information (data gathering)
6. Analyze the information
7. Develop an action plan-Execute the action plan
8. Identify lessons learned

COME SIT AWHILE

A Counselor's Thoughts

Come sit awhile and we shall talk
About your dreams and woes and foes,
Sit awhile and contemplate about your state of now

Let's explore the depths of who you are and
How that came to be
Explore the depths without regret of one who wants to see

To see one's self for who they are without regret or guilt
To shine your light upon the life
That wants so much to glow

Let go the past and all that's been cast
Before you came to know
That you are here and here is now

And that's all one needs to know...............................

Sierra "The Morning Star"

A COUNSELOR'S THOUGHTS

I wrote this poem as a summary for a paper I had written in regards to the study of psychological schools of thought. My professor was not impressed. She returned the paper and asked me to write a more scientific summary. This was my first poem.

The poem is related to several different psychologists and their practice of psychology. The dream interpretation is related to Freud's method of psychoanalysis. Carl Jung also valued dreams as insights into a person's psyche. Carl Rogers developed the person-centered psychological method based on positive regard for the self. He was greatly influenced by Otto Rank's interpersonal "here and now" therapy. Rank had been a close colleague of Freud. It seems to me Carl Rogers also interjected the existential concepts of seeing oneself for who they are, letting go of the past and being in the now into his theory of person-centered therapy.

Gestalt psychology probably has the greatest impact on this poem. Gestalt psychology is laced with ancient Eastern Philosophies and religious concepts which include existentialism.

Gestalt psychology and therapy is an outgrowth of the work of many psychologists such as: Otto Rank and his "here and now" approach; Kurt Goldstein's Holistic theory of the organism; Max Wertheimer's perception and problem solving; Jan Smuts Holism and Fritz Perls development of Gestalt Therapy. It seems to me the objective of Gestalt Therapy is to enable a person to become aware of themselves, how they got to be who they are, then let all the baggage go, and remove the blocks to resolve unfinished issues with the knowledge they are free to create a future of optimum satisfaction, fulfillment and growth.

Perls' poem below sums up his feelings in regards to Gestalt psychology.

Reality is nothing but
The sum of all the awareness
As you experience here and now
The ultimate of science thus appears
As Husserl's unit of phenomenon
And Ehrenfeld's discovery:
The irreducible phenomenon of all
Awareness, the one he named
And we still call
GESTALT.
(Perls, 1969b, p.30)

Someone I'll Come to Know

The candles were all lit and standing in a row
The music whispered softly
He's someone you'll come to know

Across the room our eyes met deeply and serene
We stared into each other's
Hoping not to make a scene

I thought this odd and wondered
What his role would be
As time and distance wandered would he be with me?

The night was long and crowded
There was too much going on
For us to know each other the journey would be long

And as this journey travels hither-to-and fro
The question still unanswered
Is he someone I'll come to know?

Now destiny eludes us, but time will come to
show If he's the one I've searched for
If he's someone I'll come to know

Sierra "The Morning Star"

SOME ONE I'LL COME TO KNOW

This is about those times when you make eye contact with someone across a crowded room. The type of eye contact that makes you wonder, hmmm, wonder if. Especially if you're available and open for a relationship and if you know you're going to see this person across the room many times. This is not a one-time occurrence.

This poem is about knowing you can place yourself across the room from this person at will. You don't have to wait for an opportunity you can create the opportunity. Then you have to decide if this is something you really want to explore, do you really want to know if a relationship is possible with this person. Perhaps the fantasy is better than reality. Therefore, time and space may help determine how you really feel and if this relationship is something you would consider in your everyday life.

Most of the time the fantasy is better!

First Glance

Upon first glance there was a chance
That this was meant to be
For he held my glance and with that stance
We drew closer to proceed

His hair was blonde and curly
His eyes were bright and blue
His body young and virile
Was this all a clue?

The star lit night was anxious
The moon was shining bright
And lips began to dance
Beneath this starry moonlight site

The kiss was lit with passion
The way a kiss should be
But should these two be sharing
What may never be meant to be?

Alas the kiss has ended
And they've gone their separate ways
But starlit nights remember the dance that might've stayed

Sierra "The Morning Star"

FIRST GLANCE

He was so cute! Blonde, athletic, blue eyes ah yes, all the makings of someone that interests me. We were committee members of a work-related professional organization but worked for different divisions of the corporation.

We had great fun together but it was not meant for us to spend too much time together. We watched the Cassini launch from the beach and had lots of hot passionate moments in lots of places.

But as life goes so goes that which is not our destiny.

Embrace

Around my waist his arm he placed
And mine upon his shoulders laced
All in a place as many times before

My hands flew up my body back
My soul eyes opened wide
As etheric stars burst forth from his heart and from mine

He held me tight as our souls came forth into each other's arms
And I looked around inside this place and
Marveled at this snowy space

As I glanced down, I caught a glimpse of iridescent robes
That entered through his body
To join us in the throws

My soul took flight with this white light
And as it joined with other exploded in divine embrace
An experience like no other

My body now began to feel and as my eyes did open,
I saw my soul pulled into me
With every cell awoken!

I felt his cheek upon mine heavy with embrace
The divine I had experienced with
Infinite loving grace

The love it stayed for several days for which I was elated
But when it past I was aghast
At the emptiness that awaited

Sierra "The Morning Star"

EMBRACE

I attended a spiritual conference in July of 2003. I was familiar with some of the people at the conference and had established a friendly relationship with several others. I had attended several seminars/workshops provided by this organization and the same channeler. This particular group of people did a lot of organizational related greeting and departing hugging; nothing intimate or sexual just in good stead. I had hugged this particular channeler many, many times. It was just what we all did.

After the channel was over and I had gone to dinner with at that time someone I considered a friend. Someone I considered trustworthy; someone I thought I could share my spiritual experiences with and have the discussion remain confidential. As the story goes, I was wrong.

We came back from dinner and entered the ballroom where everyone was buying books and other conference related items. I saw the channeler and went over to hug him as I had many, many times before, but to my amazement when I put my arms around his neck and our heart centers touched, my soul eyes opened wide, I felt the starburst in my chest only this time I saw my soul walk out of my body into the arms of the soul of the person I was hugging. Our souls were iridescent, mine was dressed in a pink flowing robe with glittering gold trim and my hair was long wavy and golden red; he was clothed in white pants and white tunic top with a gold rope type fixture surrounding his body that sat on his hips. Our souls merged into one. I was looking around and we were snowy like static on a TV, as I was glancing down at my hand and thinking this was so cool, I saw a being in white iridescent robes walk into his body from behind. This being pulled me close and a tremendous force carried us (not sure who) upward toward the most beautiful bright white light I have ever seen. I could see more bright white light above me and outlines of other beings, many beings. Then the bright white light that was holding me and me became one with the other bight white light and there was this tremendous explosion of bright white light. It felt wonderful! Then I felt a sharp little pain just below my collar bone and I thought I wonder what that is? Then I opened my eyes and saw my soul being pulled back into every cell in my body. I could feel the cheek of the person I was hugging lying heavily on my face I couldn't move for several minutes. Then I let go of him and he continued to hug others.

For days afterwards I had this feeling of divine love in my chest. It was an incredible feeling! The experience had been one of divine love filling me completely. When this feeling of complete love left me, I felt completely disconnected from everything. I felt as if it would've been possible for me to walk right through the veil body and all. One day in the fall of 2003 my 6-year-old grandson took my hand and looked me in the eye and with his sweet little voice said to me remember grandma and he sang to me the verse "a whole new world for you and me" "remember grandma". It was at that point I began to reconnect. I don't know how he knew to sing that verse to me.

I was relentless trying to find out what had happened but to no avail to this day I'm not really sure what happened in those few seconds, in the middle of a well-lit ballroom surrounded by hundreds of people. No one else was aware of what had just taken place. The person I experienced this with to this day will not discuss with me what happened or if he knows, or I don't even know how much of this he experienced or was witness to by his soul eyes. The best I've gotten from him is that I had an incredible experience not to let anyone ever take it away from me.

21

I shared this experience with a person I thought was a friend and one other person from this organization I thought was a friend. The result of sharing this divine experience with the first person resulted in a disagreement between us that somehow exploded unfavorably for me into the organization. The other person I shared the experience and argument information with also betrayed my confidence which also filtered into the organization.

The outcome of having shared this incredible experience with people I trusted resulted in the biggest disappointment of my life, mostly because these people consider themselves to be highly evolved spiritually.

Grandson

He is love
He is light
He is sunshine, he is might

He is thoughtful
He is kind
He's always on my mind

He is curious
He is clever
He's a student now and forever

He looks forward to each day
In the most pleasant of ways
He's an ace, he's the first, charming and alert

He likes people
He likes song
He always tries to get along

He is talented
He is smart
And I cherish him with all my heart, for

He's an angel full of grace, and none can take his place

Sierra "The Morning Star"

GRANDSON

He was a special little being when he was born. He was born 9 weeks early. The doctor tried to stop the labor but was unsuccessful. He was 3.5 pounds at birth but he never seemed that little. He was very long. He spent the first month in an incubator at Arnold Palmer Hospital for Children. He was moved to a local hospital and spent two more months in an encapsulated crib until he weighed 4 pounds.

He was growing up just fine, we were always very close but his mom kept saying she thought something wasn't right. He and I always communicated perfectly, I didn't realize he was having a difficult time communicating with other people, including his mother. I always knew what he wanted and he always looked me in the eye.

His test diagnosis was high functioning Autism accompanied by a Language Processing Disorder. We got him into specialized training early.

I was able to get his mother to allow me to raise him, beginning when he was 8 years old.

His teachers at school always referred to the purity of his soul. He is very smart. He has come a long way in his ability to synthesize information and reading comprehension. He has always been very good with numbers, patterns, maps and spelling. He has always loved to read and his pronunciation/diction is very good.

Computers are easy for him. His speech and personal interactions improved as he matured. He attended regular school and learned how to make friends and what it means to be a friend. He developed a love for music!

He graduated Summa Cum Laude from Berklee College of Music, a part of the Boston Conservatory of Music, in Boston, MA.

Granddaughter

She is kind
She is sweet
And she sparkles when she sleeps

She's a flirt
She's a rogue
And she loves to powder her nose

She has style
She has grace
And she's always in a race

She makes-up songs
She makes-up dance
And oh, how she loves to prance!

She is bad
She is good
But listens mostly as she should

She loves her mom and treats her right
She loves her Bro's but likes to fight
But with her and Grandma things are often tight

But she will learn to do what's right
Even if it takes great might
To steer her from her current plight

Sierra "The Morning Star"

G R A N D D A U G H T E R

Heavy sigh! What a piece of work! She's so cute! Everyone says she looks just like me and she does. She was always into everything she would not sit still; she loved all the girly things; make-up, finger- nail polish, lip stick, eye shadow, flirting with the boys. She liked to fight with her brothers until they fought back. I would tell her you get as good as you give. She liked to climb trees and wrestle too!

She's did not do well in school because she was too busy watching what everyone else was doing, what they were saying, what they were wearing. It seems she also has a learning disability which has never been diagnosed. That could have been what caused the distractions.

We were hopeful she would end up in Hollywood or New York City where her singing, dancing, flare for color and other artistic behaviors would have been appreciated.

Sad to say things did not go that way. She and her younger brother ended up being raised by a father that was mean, angry, resentful and abusive, both psychologically and physically. As a result, she has grown up with little self-worth.

Her behavior was so bad in elementary school (when she was living with her dad) she was assigned to a special class room, one where no teaching occurred. As a result, she never learned to read, or do math or science or anything you learn in elementary school. To my knowledge no testing was ever done to discern what disability she may have and to this day she struggles with everyday life and everyday decision making. However, she thinks she knows everything and will not follow directions unless they benefit her immediate needs.

Grandson 2

He is deep
He is dark
And he is often distraught

His knee-high world
Was quick to find
He didn't understand all of the time

He was small
He was strong
And he strived to move along

He missed his mom and
Longed for hope
That his love would not be jerked

That he would grow to impose
The love he knows he'd turn to gold

Sierra "The Morning Star"

GRANDSON 2

He's the youngest and did really well with keeping up with the older two especially his sister since they are the closest in age. They were always about the same height when they were young but he weighed more. He's built like a linebacker so when she fought with him, he usually won even though he was younger.

Although he could keep-up physically with the other two and intellectually a head of his sister, emotionally he's the baby of the family. His mom and dad not living together was the most emotionally difficult on him. He cried easily. Being the youngest seemed to be difficult for him. I was the youngest but, it was always easier for me.

He struggled to understand what was really going on with his home life. He did well in school unlike his sister. However, when he reached Senior High School things got bad for him. There were gangs at his school in Charlotte, NC and he got him-self in trouble.

I think he has learned his lesson and will be able to move forward successfully.

Daughter

Her hopes and dreams are never set
She wanders through
With much regret

Goals and schedules not her pleasure
Vanquish hopes of finding treasure
Treasure hidden deep with-in to activate for the win

The treasure of self-worth to find
Hidden deep with-in the mine
If only if she'd find the map, to lead her to the scared path

She seeks the treasure here not blind
Self-worth will bring her from behind
If only she would try to find

The path that leads her through the mine

Sierra "The Morning Star"

DAUGHTER

I have a beautiful daughter. She is clever, personable and, outgoing. She saw herself as the unique person she was, however she was insistent her way was correct and she was entitled not to follow the rules the rest of world had to live by. If she were queen of the universe or lived on an isolated island this concept would have complemented her life. Much to her dismay she was not the queen of the universe nor did she live on an isolated deserted island.

She still struggles with racial prejudice with regards to her choice of companionship and her children. At the age of 30 she finally began to grasp the concept if she wanted to move forward with life, she had to accept the status quo and work with in it, to change her life from the inside out. If not, she would not be able to move beyond to where she wanted to be.

I think this is the fundamental lesson we all learn, but at different stages and to varying degrees in our journey each life time on this planet.

She is 46 now, and has learned the lessons life has to teach, her way, which was the difficult path. She has made the path correction and is pursuing her dreams.

Creativity

Creativity is pink,
Creativity is yellow,
Creativity abounds
In every hue and color

Creativity is math,
Creativity is science,
Creativity is life,
In every size, shape and color

Creativity is form,
Creativity is function,
Creativity unfolds
At all life's junctures

Creativity is subtle,
Creativity is bold,
Creativity surrounds us
Where ever we may go

Creativity is song,
Creativity is dance,
Creativity is movement,
Through life's advance

Sierra "The Morning Star"

CREATIVITY

This poem was initiated by a discussion that ensued at a meeting as to the limits of creativity. Obviously to me creativity has no bounds. Everything is a thought before it becomes a concrete reality. Sometimes the thought becoming a concrete reality is limited by time, money or general support therefore the reality is not as creative as the original thought but none the less becomes part of our three D existence.

The Glow

Death as Life spawns a new
Departed from what once we knew
Neither space without embrace
But each space a different place.

Each a space we come to know
With eyes wide open we see The Glow
The Glow that shines upon our face
The Glow we trust and embrace.

A Glow of life in different space,
A Glow of life to embrace
The Glow of life eternal place,
Dawns a new each time and space.

Sierra "The Morning Star"

THE GLOW

This was written for a co-worker. We had just started working on a project when his father was first hospitalized. During the course of the project his father was in and out of the hospital and nursing home for about six months before he died. The poem is about living and dying and not remembering this side of the veil when we're over there and then when we go back, we soon forget about life on this side of the veil and then we come back again.

Each side of the veil is a place with experiences to embrace. We feel the glow of the sun on this side of the veil and the glow of divine love on the other side of veil, although sometimes we can feel the glow of divine love on this side of the veil. The question is can we feel the sun's glow on the other side of the veil?

The In-Between

In-between you and me
Lies a place beyond this space
In-between you and me
Is a space to believe-in and investigate

To reach the space you must embrace
The all of you in this place
The space that is beyond this place
A space to refresh and make you, you again

You again to face this world
You again with stories yet unknown
You again to dance a new
You again to join life's crew

Sierra "The Morning Star"

THE IN-BETWEEN

This is not a concrete place but a place to rejuvenate. A space to escape too that doesn't cost money and no one else is there with you. It's a space where you are there with you, a space to contemplate what's true for you. This is somewhere most are not aware exist. They don't believe in it or investigate the possibility and therefore can't get to it.

It seems to me if more people would work on getting to this space and spending some time in it, there might be a little more clarity in this place.

Dreams

Dreams are made for us to keep
Dreams are there as we sleep
Dreams are where we all meet to share the night as we sleep

Dreams can take us far away
Dreams can take us to the play
The play of life of day to day

For dreams are life
And dreams are love
Dreams are a gift from above

So, dream each night and escape
Dream each night and then awake
Awake each dawn to renew the gift of life for me and you

Sierra "The Morning Star"

DREAMS

Dreams are a space where we express our fear and our passion without consequence. Dreams allow us to experience what if situations. They help us release anxiety and release suppressed thoughts and feelings yet it doesn't seem to me most of us use this state of consciousness as a release valve. To me dreams have the ability to aide emotional healing and visit those we miss and converse with those we need to discuss issues with. Perhaps there needs to be a dream school so we can all take advantage of this wonderful state of consciousness.

Bubbles

Bubbles, bubbles everywhere
Bubbles floating in the air
Iridescent with no care

Bubbles take bad thoughts away
Bubbles bring me thoughts that play,
And help me through the day to day

Bubbles, bubbles everywhere
Bubbles, bubbles take my cares,
Bubble, bubbles here and there

To help me through all I dare

Sierra "The Morning Star"

BUBBLES

Bubbles, was written for my oldest grandson. He worries about everything sometimes consuming him. I wrote the poem to help him send his worrying thoughts away and fill him with light airy colorful feelings. Hopefully bubble thoughts will help him discover how to control what he thinks about.

Wander

We wander here
We wander there
We wander round and through to where?

To where there's joy
To where there's pleasure
To where the light has hid the treasure

To see what's here
To see what's there
But do we see how much we care?

We care for those that wander there
We care for those who come to share
The care that makes us more aware

Aware of wonder from here to there.......

Sierra "The Morning Star"

WANDER

Wander is about the traveling I've done all my life, this unsettled feeling of wander and wonder. Something about me likes to wander and all of me is full of wonder! I would like to create a home as I haven't felt like I've had one since my father and sister died when I was 11 (1965). Home has been illusive to me. I've tried to create it many places with many different people but it never feels like home, the home I miss the home I remember. I've owned five houses one with each husband and three on my own. I would really love to have a home that feels like home, but I haven't figured out the formula yet.

Perhaps the home my heart is remembering is not a place on this planet it's home on the other side of the veil, the home that is home to all of us in between life times and that's why I can't create it here, because it's there. But is seems to me I should be able to duplicate it here.

Wander includes my metaphysical travels and travels to the in-between. These travels keep me close to my spiritual home, the awareness of being here and there and, trying to create the home feeling here the same as there.

I now own my fifth home and it is the finest house I have ever owned or lived in. Who knows where my travels will take me to, next!

The Circle's Won

At last, I glance upon the face
Of time forgot and space displaced

A glance of what was meant to be
A chance for all eternity

A chance to move beyond old space,
and create,
a place for unity

A unity once now forgot
Is now about to be brought

Brought back together once again
Brought back together there is no end

For male and female once undone
Join now again the circle's won!

Sierra "The Morning Star"

THE CIRCLE'S WON

This poem is about the concept, once upon a time male and female energy was one, a whole. The energy split a part to learn about "all that is". The split was into male and female energy to experience the learning from different aspects. Two opposite parts could learn more than one part, double the experience, double the knowledge in a shorter amount of time, and then come back together again to synthesize the experience.

EPILOGUE

Remembering............it seems that's what I've been trying to do for as long as I can remember. Searching for answers, trying to understand what I'm searching for, what I'm trying to find, what is it I'm trying to remember that I can't seem to find?

History has always fascinated me especially ancient world history; culture, language, architecture, artifacts, government, foreign policy, politics and especially religion. Perhaps this is all directly related to me being an ancient (not sure what that means except besides I've been here thousands of life times). I have always been very comfortable with the ancient historical information I studied, it felt good, it felt correct, like an old shoe, very familiar, especially the ancient mystery schools and theology.

This is the time I've been told that the remembering will occur. I wonder what I will remember? How will the remembering come about? What will happen after I remember? Will I remember more of what I already know? Will I remember past life times? Will I remember the scared teachings of the universe? Is that what I've been searching for, the knowledge of the scared teachings? Or perhaps it's about remembering what I came here to do this life time.

I have known since I was a child there was more going on here than others are aware. I was in my late thirties before I realized most others were not aware. Then I began trying to figure out why they weren't aware. Was it because they didn't want to be, because it was easier not to? I began to understand it was about soul evolvement. I learned it was the choice of the soul to evolve, and establish the level to ascend to. No one can reach down and pull you up by the hair, and there is no judgment about the level of evolvement you attain, you just are and it's okay.

I have learned we are all here to work through our evolvement process. That we take different paths, so the journey for each of us each life time is different. I have learned that's what the planet earth was created for. What we are trying to do on a soul level is ascend. Not in the traditional sense the Christian religion supports but to ascend to the level of remembering.

The something that was in the que was the Quantum Leap, which occurred on September 18, 2007, ushering in New Energy Consciousness.

I have learned there is an essence of pain that doesn't go away but it's okay, as long as every morning you put both feet on the floor and begin each day a new, because the only way out is through.

REFERENCES

1. Perls, F.S. In and Out the Garbage Pail. Lafayette, California: Real People Press, 1969b; New York: Bantam Books, 1972.

AUTHOR'S COMMENTS

My search for the truth has led me to many paths, some that can be seen in the physical realms some seen only in the metaphysical realms. The Journey can be compared to a combination of every roller coaster ride in existence. It is exhilarating, it's frightening, it moves fast at times, slow at others, it climbs it plummets, moves from one stage to another, it twist and turns, right, left, upside down, backwards, in the tunnel, out in the sun, but always in an upward spiral and always with other souls. It is the Journey of ascension, that which truly is and always will be.

There are those who like to say the truth is different for everyone, but it seems to me there is one truth from which many value judgments are ascertained and the value judgment which best suits you is dependent on the ascended soul level you have reached.

Soul evolvement is a choice and there are no judgments in regards to the soul level you achieve. Soul evolvement is the choice of the soul and the level reached in accordance with the will of each soul for this is the Creator's gift, to the "I am".

The human experience is a configured whole of interrelated experiences and relationships. The soul and the human exist together as a configured whole. They are not separate they are one. The soul is divine the human is the vessel for the soul to learn and experience the lessons of accession. The Holy Spirit gifts us the blessing of eternal life, the ultimate gift of accession.

www.ingramcontent.com/pod-product-compliance
Lightning Source LLC
Chambersburg PA
CBHW051242120626
46547CB00014B/1753